Another Chance
Inspirational Poems, Songs & Testimonies

By

Dorothy A. Cooper

Another Chance

Volume I

Inspirational Poems, Songs & Testimonies

Copyright © January 2014

Dorothy A. Cooper

Dorothy A. Cooper is published under the umbrella

Of

Katrinasworks.com

Dedication

FROM THE HEART

*To my wonderful sister, Sheri Brown, and her awesome husband, Anthony Brown, I now take the time to dedicate, in their honor, **Another Chance**.*

At my weakest moment, these two gifted souls, reached into their hearts and welcomed me in to their dwellings without any reservations. The many nights of praying for me, singing with me, reading God's most Holy words with me, is the reason I am where I am today. Thank You Father God, I say, for placing such diligent servants in my presence! Their Kingdom Works are too many to name Father, but, it is my prayer blessings are bestowed upon for all of their unselfish labor. I love the two of you tremendously.

To my five children, Aris, Adidus, Anshel, Ansheneike, Ashayla, and especially my two twin granddaughters, many thanks to each of you for staying focused on the positive while your Mother was going through a very difficult time. I know it had to have been hard to see me suffer, but, as you see now, it was all for God's glory. Hallelujah! I love each of you so very much and am just as equally proud. I ask, however, no matter what, each of you keep making your Mom proud by representing God first! ***Another Chance,*** *I also dedicate to each of you as well.*

To my parents, Jessie and Fannie Dyson, words cannot express how much love I harbor in my heart for each of you. My prayer is one day to be able to show you and not just tell you! To the rest of my siblings, Jessie Jr, Berda, Jerry, Edward, Casey, and especially Delone (deceased), thank you and I love you!

Finally, to every last one of my nieces, nephews, aunts, uncles, cousins and dear friends (John, Na'eem, Barbara, Sar Rahdahfeeyahu, Vernon, and Herb) I love you all so much!

Thank you for your support! Amen...

Lord, I Surrender All Unto You.....
September 26, 2011

REBAPTISM IN THE NAME OF JESUS
…..the day my life changed "for the good of them who love the Lord." {Romans 8:28}

Officiating Pastors
My Sister and Brother-in-law
Brother & Sister Anthony and Sheri Brown

Another Chance

ANOTHER CHANCE

So many questions, Jesus

Roaming through my mind.

Been looking for answers,

But they seem too hard to find.

How did I get in this empty place?

Why must there be so much pain?

Please forgive me, Jesus;

And give me another chance!

Cause with another chance Lord Your will I vow to obey!

Yes, with another chance, Jesus, I vow to do whatever You say!

Cause apparently; it's best to be, obedient to the plans You made for me!

So please forgive me Father and give me another chance!

Cause right now, I'm broken Master –

All of my strength is just about gone!

Feeling so hopeless, Master –

Trying to figure out what I did wrong!

I'm down on bended knees

Crying Lord, forgive me please!

I'm asking You, Father,

To give me another chance!

AN ENCOUNTER WITH THE LORD

In the midst of the quietness, silence suddenly whispers.
Causing turbulence to stir up the warmness of the blood;
Which freely flows, throughout the veins; like a flood.
Then, trembling begins, from deep within, the soul;
Bringing the weight of the frame, to its knees,
As the membrane ponders, please.
What is this feeling triumphing over me?
Am I dying? Why am I suddenly crying?
With each tick tock, however, of the clock,
The breathing begins to go array; and the frame of the body
Volunteers to sway, from side to side!
Making it difficult, not to oblige!

It seems uncontrollable, yes it does,
Quite contrary; in fact, even somewhat scary,
For now, there is a voice; not of my choice!
Speaking a foreign language from the tongue;
As screams are being exalted from the lungs:
Hallelujah! Passing through, every now and then,
Helps the fear to understand,
This spirit, which now controls me, is Holy;
And cannot be denied!
For it is all because of the love; dwelling deep inside,
For my Father; yes, which art in heaven!

Thank you, at this point, is what I extend: over and over again.
    While clapping my hands,
    For, in the end, the spirit becomes renewed
    And the flesh, somehow, subdued
    Because of this encounter, just experienced
    With the Lord! Amen!

Because Of My Faith

There's been days I could not see.
The pain was so unbearable,
It lead to nights I could not sleep.

But I held on;
I stayed strong!
I made it through the storm,
Because of my faith!

Because of my faith, I made it!
Because of my faith, I made it!
God gave me another chance
So I placed all my trials in His hands
I made it through the storm
Because of my faith!

So glad God was there to listen
To the troubles I was going through
Many times wanted to give up
But He gave me strength to endure!

So I held on;
I stayed strong!
I made it through the storm,
Because of my faith!

Because of my faith, I made it!
Because of my faith, I made it!
God gave me another chance
So I placed all my trials in His hands
I made it through the storm,
Because of my faith!

BEYOND THE SKY

Beyond the sky;
I shall fly, some day.
Like an eagle soaring,
Way up high!

I shall spread my wings,
And fly away to glory!
One day beyond the sky!

I'm living my life.
Changing wrongs to right.
Cause I want to be ready;
When it's time to take my flight.

I want to be able,
To hear the angels sing!
While sitting on the right hand of the King
Some day beyond the sky!

Beyond the sky!
Beyond the sky I shall fly!
One day beyond the sky!

Oh, beyond the sky;
I shall fly, some day!
Like an eagle soaring;
Way up high!

I shall spread my wings;
And fly away to glory!
Some day,
One day;
Beyond the sky!

By Calling On Jesus

By calling on Jesus in the morning!
By calling on Jesus in the evening!
By calling on Jesus all night long too,
It's something I really love to do;
From day to day because
By calling on Jesus is how I make it through!

Jesus, in the morning!
Jesus, in the evening!
Jesus, all night long too!
Jesus, from day to day!
Won't have it any other way!
Because Jesus is how I make it through!

CAST YOUR CARES UPON THE LORD

Cast your cares upon the Lord
And leave them right there.
Cast your cares upon the Lord
And leave them right there.

All of your burdens
All of your fears
All of trials
Every last one of your tears

Cast your cares upon the Lord,
And leave them right there
Cast your cares upon the Lord
And leave them right there

All of your sleepless nights
Because of situations not going right;
All of your weary days
Because of having no strength to fight!

Cast your cares upon the Lord!
Cast your cares upon the Lord!
Cast your cares upon the Lord!
And leave them right there!

Cause believer when you do
Jesus will deliver you
From what you're going through
So cast your cares upon the Lord

CHANGE ALL OF ME

I gave You my heart Lord
So You could change its beat
I gave You my mind Lord
So You could change how it thinks

From the crown of my head
All the way down to the soles of my feet
I place in Your hands
So You can change all of me

All of me
All of me, sweet Jesus
I place in Your hands
So You can change
All of me (repeat twice)
(back to top)

Come Bow Down At The Alter

At the alter
You can come bow down
And leave there secrets kept
From down through the years

Cause at the alter
The unknown record shared
Will be left safe in the hollow
Of the Redeemer's ears

At the alter
Pain gets destroyed
As tears

I've been suffering a great deal
For a long, long time
Some days pain was so unbearable
Until

Lord, if I could only touch
The hem of your garment
Then all of my issues
Would be subdued

Come Free My Soul

Come; free my soul

Unchain the hollow space of darkness;

Which hovers constantly within;

Like a rotating cloud blowing ever so gently in the wind.

Make peace be still, by occupying its walls,

With the elaborate color of your being.

For it is you. The only one who can

Fill emptiness' fears and loneliness' tears.

Come; free my soul.

Rearrange things, so the change brings

Repetitious praises unto your name.

As patience and silence entertains me; however

While the tock of the clock,

Chimes musically in my ears;

Rest assured, for unyielding faith says,

Soon you will appear.

Then I shall behold your story

For the rest of eternity.

But, until then, with opened arms;

I shall continue to wait.

Anxiously; curiously; but humbly,

No matter how much time it takes. I shall wait.

So, come; free my soul

No need to knock when you get here

For you are the key….

COVER ME LORD

On this cold fall night,
Cover me Lord.
Wrap my tiredness up,
Until the security felt;
Slowly begins to make
All discomfort melt.
Rejuvenate my weary bones;
As the warmth of Your touch;
Causes a satisfying moan.
Cover me Lord;
On this cold fall night!
Let Your Light; like a blanket,
Fall gently upon me.
From the crown of my head,
To the sole of my feet.
Cover me Lord!
Cradle me; tight as
A couple's spoon -
Leaving no room;
For anything, which
May cause gloom.
In order for tomorrow to find my best;
Tonight my body must rest! Therefore;
Cover me Lord;

On this cold fall night!

EVERY KNEE SHALL BOW

There shall come a time
In our lives
When every voice shall cry out
Unto Christ

Oh, there will come a day
When our way
Will make us cry out
And seek His grace

Cause every knee shall bow (Bow down)
Every knee shall bow (Bow down and give God praise)
Oh, every knee shall bow (Bow down)
Bow down and give God praise (Bow down and give God praise)

It does not matter who or what you are
Every tongue shall confess unto God
That He is the way
Yes, Lord You are the way

Oh and there shall come a time in our lives
Where every voice shall cry out unto Christ
Lord, help me please
Have mercy on me, please

Oh, cause every knee shall bow (Bow down)
Every knee shall bow (Bow down and give God praise)
Yes, every knee shall bow (Bow down)
Bow down and give God praise (Bow down and give

God praise)
Bow down and give God praise (Bow down and give God praise)

FOR MY FAMILY

For my family
I fought through the dark
For my family
I fought there all alone
Some days it was so cloudy
But I kept right on fighting
For my family
Could one day be free!

For my family
I gave up everything
For my family
Many sacrifices have been made
But I would do it all again
If it meant another chance
For my family
Could one day be free!

I endured so much pain
But I would do it all again
For my family
Could one day be free!

GLORY UNTO OUR KING

Woke up this morning
Feeling great
For it's a new day
To shout glory unto our King

Because of His mercy
Because of His grace
I've got another chance
To shout glory unto our King

It's a new day (To shout glory)
It's a new day (To shout glory)
I've got another chance (To shout glory)
Glory unto our King (Unto our King)

For while I was sleep
By my side You never left me
Glory (Unto our King)
Glory (Unto our King)

For shielding me in Your arms
For covering me with Your blood
I've got to shout glory (Unto our King)
I've got to shout glory (Unto our King)

Glory (Glory)
Glory (Glory)
Glory (Glory)
Unto our King (Unto Our King)

For being the only one there

When no one else seemed to care
Glory (Glory)
Glory (Glory)
Glory (Glory)
Unto our King (Unto our King)
Unto our King (Unto our King)
Unto our King (Unto our King)
Glory unto our King (Unto our King)

GOD BROKE THE CHAINS OFF OF ME

I remember the days
When I felt bound in sin
My soul was so lost
Didn't know how it would all end

But I prayed and prayed
Kept my mind on the Lord
Now I'm getting
My reward

Cause God broke the (Chains off, chains off, chains off of me)
God broke the (Chains off, chains off, chains off of me)
See the more I praised Him
Deep in me God made a change
And that's how He broke the chains off of me

Oh I remember the time
I almost lost my mind
For peace from all my problems
Was so hard to find

But on my knees I stayed
And I prayed and prayed
Now I'm getting
My reward

Cause God broke the chains off, chains off, chains off of me
Cause God broke the chains off, chains off, chains off of me

The more I praised Him
Deep in me God made a change
And that's how He broke the chains off of me

Now I can praise God, praise God, praise God freely
Yes, I can praise God, praise God, praise God freely
Oh, the more I praise Him
The more blessings I receive
And that's how He broke the chains off of me

I GIVE ALL PRAISE UNTO OUR KING

I give all praise unto our King!
For His Amazing Grace!
Oh and for His mercy!
I give all praise unto our King!

His mercy endures forever!
His glory endures forever!

I give all praise!
I give all praise!
I give all praise!
Unto our King!

I MADE IT

Had some hard times
Living was so tough
Had some dark days
Felt like giving up

But I'm here today
Oh Lord, giving You praise
Cause I made it
I made it

So many sleepless nights
Next day had no fight
But in the back of my mind
Something kept telling me things were gonna be alright
Oh and the loss of loved ones
Left so much pain in my heart
But I held on
Somehow I stayed strong

And I made it
I, made it
Oh, Oh, Thank God I made it
Thank You God I made it through
Now I can live on
I can face any storm

So many times I wanted to give up
Of trials and tribulations I had enough
But I cried and prayed
Prayed and cried

That's why I'm standing here today
Oh Lord, giving You praise
'Cause I made it
I made it through

THANKS TO GOD I AM FREE

No more worries,
No more fears.
Thanks to God Almighty
I am free!

No more pain,
No more tears.
Thanks to God Almighty
I am free!

Free from situations,
Free from tribulations;
Free from desolation to.
Thanks to God Almighty.
I am free!

Cause when lost in a world of sin
The Lord came and took me by my hand
Told me everything would be okay
Then He showed me a better way

Now, thanks to God Almighty

I am free!

I am free!

I am free!

Thanks to God Almighty,

I am free!

In The Eyes Of The Beholder

In the eyes of the Beholder
Is where I long to be!
Wrapped up in His favor;
Where there is nothing but peace!
Cause in the eyes of the Beholder
There is no worries!

In the eyes of the Beholder;
In the eyes of the Beholder
In the eyes of the Beholder;
Is where I long to be!

This way, He can see my iniquities!
This way, He can keep His eyes on me!
How much I enjoy giving Him praise!
How much I enjoy calling on His name!

In the eyes of the Beholder;
In the eyes of the Beholder;
In the eyes of the Beholder;
Is where I long to be!
Hallelujah!

MAKE US OVER LORD

Lord, cradle us in Your arms;
As You bathe us with Your blood.
Then dress us with Your love.
As You make us over, Lord!

Change our sinful ways;
Until they resemble faith.
So our thoughts can line up with Yours;
Oh! Make us over, Lord!

Yes, make us over!
We need You to make us over Lord!
This is personal! Yea! Yea!

So Your way is what is seen.
Destroy all iniquities!
So we can all come together
And Your praises we shall sing!

Yes, make us over!
We need You to make us over Lord!
This is personal! Yea! Yea!

ONE STEP CLOSER TO THE LORD

Every step that we take

Every sacrifice that we make

Gets us one step closer

To the Lord

Every test that we pass

Every storm we outlast

Gets us one step closer

To the Lord

Every step that we take

Every sacrifice that we make

Gets us one step closer

To the Lord

Every test that we pass

Every storm we outlast

Gets us one step closer

To the Lord

Gets us one step closer

To the Lord

(CHORUS)

Every time we say Amen

Every time we lift up our hands

It puts us one step closer to the Lord

Every time we shout out for joy

Oh! The enemy is destroyed

And we are one step closer to the Lord (go back to top)

Oh! Closer to the Lord

I want to be	Ohhhhh! I want to be closer
Closer to the Lord	I want to be closer
I want to be	Closer to You Lord
Closer to the Lord	I want to be closer

I want to be   Closer to You Master

Closer to the Lord

I want to be

Closer (Closer)

Closer (Closer)

Closer (Closer)

Closer (Closer) (I want to be)

(for conclusion repeat 1st 2 verses)

ONLY THING LEFT WAS TO PRAY

Trapped in desolation
Feelings of desperation
Only thing left was to pray
Hard to understand
How this could be in God's plan
Only thing left was to pray

So down on bended knees
Said Lord help me please
Show me thy ways
Cause in order to make it through
I know I must turn to You
So teach me Lord how to pray

Three o'clock in the morn
In my life became the norm
There was no one in the room, Lord
With me, but You
The Word constantly in my sight
Brought me out of the darkness
Into the marvelous Light
When the only thing left was to pray

So, down on bended knees
Said Lord, help me please
Show me thy ways
Cause in order to make it through
I know I must turn to You
So teach me Lord how to pray

Staying down on bended knees
Saying Lord help me please
I'm a witness, is the answer to making it through
Cause God's Amazing Grace
Showed a sinner like me the way
When the only thing left was to pray!

Oh yes, the Lord's presence
Truly changed my life
And all that was going wrong
Started to go right
When the only thing left was to pray!

PERFECTION

For the most part; Perfection comes in all different
Sizes, colors, and even shapes. It is not sold,
At a price to be paid for with money. For,
Perfection endured the price, just too unselfishly
Be the example of Divine Perfection. Perfection;
However, is the very reason, it is literally earned
Through the shedding of blood, sweat, and tears,
But, needless to say; derives, also, therefore, through
The endurance of much pain brought on, most times;
By the ill-gotten ways, of peers who have
Perfected the art of hindrance.

By the way, one, unexpectedly, just does not wake
One day, bearing his or her cross in the middle of Perfection,
Unless, perhaps; he, she, or even it; in some cases,
Has endured the process of elimination -
In which it takes, that is, to not just walk like,
But; to, coincidentally, be raised to resemble Perfection.
Much submissive labor; and considerable focus,
Combined with perseverance, withstanding, and yes;
Even sheer determination is without a doubt,
What makes up the perfect in Perfection!
It is all done, with time, however, to produce

A better way. Specifically, in most cases,
For the very same ones - Disregarding the unselfish
Struggles suffered in order to give birth to Perfection!

Therefore, Perfection does not boast or brag; but,
Yet in still; once obtained, brings about true inspiration!
As well as admiration, yes, from many of those
Same naysayers, who, then in turn; now gives praise
For the salvation seen! Even, unbelievably, after
Perfection's Purpose, has not just been revealed,
But fulfilled! It's okay, however, for, humbleness,
Then becomes Perfection's trophy, received.
For, the heart knows, when looking back -
At the path left leading to Perfection's blessings,
That is, none of it, could not have nor would not have;
Been possible without the sculpting and molding
From the only two hands powerful enough;
To create; Perfection!
It's why I serve thee the way I do! Amen...

PREPARE ME JESUS

Prepare me Jesus.
Season me with Your love.
Stir up all of my flavors.
So unto You, I am desirable!

Blend it all together;
With a little of Your favor!
So that the aroma,
Will be a blessing to all of my neighbors!

Add only those ingredients; Jesus,
Which will make me pleasing unto You!
So with every bite; Your taste buds,
Will shout, "um, um good"!

Place me; Preparer,
In to a temperature hot as the sun;
So when You bring me out,
You will know , I am well done!

Prepare me Jesus.
According to Your perfect recipe!
Prepare me Jesus.

So when it is all over;

With me, You are well pleased!

Prepare me Jesus!

PURGE MY HEART

Purge my heart, Lord.

Look inside it and clean it up.

Fill it with favor;

Until it runs over like a cup!

May surely, goodness and mercy;

Reside on the outside.

As Your holy presence;

Be its walls on the inside!

Purge my heart, Lord!

Purge my heart, Lord!

Purge my heart Lord.

Until it desires to follow Your way!

Tune and transform it

To beat to the rhythm of what You say!

Fill it with Your kindness!

Fill it with Your love!

Create in it newness;

As You fill it with Your blood!

Purge my heart, Lord!

Purge my heart, Lord!

Sometimes Jesus He's All We Got

When people, places, and things;
Leaves the spirit soaking in pain,
Sometimes Jesus, He's all we got.

When can't depend on anyone else,
Includes relying on ourselves;
Since in our circle everyone has left.
Sometimes Jesus, He's all we got.

Yes, sometimes Jesus, He's all we got!

Faithful to show He cares
Ready and willing to be there
Providing the cloth to catch our tears
Yes, sometimes Jesus, He's all we got!

Have you ever had to cry when trying Him?
Have you ever had to lean on His Word?
Did He come after you tried Him?
Because your sovereign prayer He heard?

Sometimes Jesus, He's all we got!

STILL GIVING PRAISE TO GOD

Til it's all said and done!
Til it's all said and done!
Til it's all said and done!
I'm gonna be the one,
Still giving praise to God!

I'm gonna praise Him with my whole heart!
I'm gonna praise Him during the day and when it's dark!
Twenty-four hours seven days a week;
You can surely find me,
Giving praise to God!

No matter what I am going through.
No matter what the enemy try to do.
Til it's all said and done;
I'm gonna be the one,
Still giving praise to God!

When you took my home,
When you took my car;
Left me down and out,
When you took my job!
But in the midst of it all,

I still was standing tall;
Giving praise to God!

Til it's all said and done!
Til it's all said and done!
Til it's all said and done!
I'm gonna be the one,
Still giving praise to God!

STRAIGHT FROM MY HEART LORD

Straight from my heart Lord;

I really love You, Yes I do!

Straight from my heart Lord;

I really love You, this is true!

Straight from my heart Lord!

All I do is thinking of You

Straight from my heart Lord;

Comes the will to serve You!

Wouldn't have it any other way!

For Your presence lights up my day!

Don't care what nobody else says!

Because You are my everything!

Yeah! Yeah! Yeah! Yeah!

SURE DO MISS YOU

It really doesn't seem fair.
Sitting, thinking about the good times shared.
Wishing somehow you would appear;
So together, we could make one more memory.
What would it be? The one more memory?
Me...holding you...for the rest of eternity!

A huge part of me, you were;
Or should I say; still is?
Sometimes, believe it or not;
As words spew from my lips:
It's your voice my ears hear.
Even the way I tilt my head; at times,
Brings about visions of you to my mind.
Can't help but to shed a tear.
For, you were definitely one of a kind.

Sorry for being so unaware of the inevitable.
How one minute you were here: then the next...
Oh well! Been striving to understand God's plan.
That is for every man born of a woman.
May be someday I will be okay.
However today, it would be nice,
Just to hear you say, "I love you!"

It's true! Not a day goes by, where in
I don't think of you! Not a night goes by,
Where when, I finally do fall to sleep,
I don't dream of you. And as soon as I wake,
My heart wonders, if somehow;
By chance; you're dreaming of me too!
Sure do miss you!

Thank God For Jesus

Jesus, bleed on a cross for me!
Jesus, went through harsh pain for me!

I could of been dead;
Sleeping in my grave.
Oh, but Jesus!
Continues to make a way!

I thank God for Jesus! (His unselfish ways saves my life!)
I thank God for Jesus! (His unselfish ways saves my life!)
His unselfish ways! (His unselfish ways saves my life!)
Saves my life! (His unselfish ways saves my life!)

Oh Jesus! (His unselfish ways saves my life!)
I thank God for Jesus! (His unselfish ways saves my life!)
Cause His unselfish ways! (His unselfish ways saves my life!)
Saves my life! (His unselfish ways saves my life!)

Saves my life! (His unselfish ways saves my life!)
Saves my life! (His unselfish ways saves my life!)
His unselfish ways; (His unselfish ways saves my life!)
Saves my life! (His unselfish ways saves my life!)

Always shielding and protecting me!

My case He continues to plead!
Even when I don't deserve it!
He still looks out for me!

I thank God for Jesus! (His unselfish ways saves my life!)
I thank God for Jesus! (His unselfish ways saves my life!)
His unselfish ways! (His unselfish ways saves my life!)
Saves my life! (His unselfish ways saves my life!)

I thank God for Jesus! (His unselfish ways saves my life!)
I thank God for Jesus! (His unselfish ways saves my life!)
His unselfish ways! (His unselfish ways saves my life!)
Saves my life! (His unselfish ways saves my life!)

THE LORD OUR GOD

(LEADER)

The Lord our God is wonderful
How excellent is thy name
O, we magnify Him
We glorify Him
For He is greatly to be praised!

(CHOIR)

The Lord our God is wonderful
How excellent is thy name
O, we magnify Him
We glorify Him
For He is greatly to be praised!

(LEADER)

Let the mountains
Skip around like rams
And the little hills
Let them skip around like lambs
As we come on one accord
Let heaven and earth rejoice
As we give reverence to our King!

(ALL)
The Lord our God is wonderful (Oh, yes He is)
How excellent is thy name (You are an awesome God)
O, we magnify Him (Glory to Your name)
We glorify Him (Hallelujah)
For He is greatly to be praised!
For He is greatly to be praised!

TOO AFRAID TO LOVE AGAIN

I want love and I want love to want me.
I want to know how it finally feels to experience the
Unmitigated thrill in which real love thrusts
In to the ramifications of life. Not the teenage
Version of puppy love, but somehow, if by chance;
The divine love, in which God ordained
Between the man and woman, which He made.
Potential love came and said he love me.
Oh, but, arrogance and fear pushed him away.
But was love really here; when so quickly he strayed?
What happened? Where did things go wrong?
Too afraid to love again.....

While sitting along in the dark writing this message,
Pain flows onto my paper from the ink of my pen.
My heart is heavy; weighted down at the fact of knowing,
All alone is what I really am and have been
For quite some time. As the darkness clouds my mind;
I want love and I want love to want me back.
But, how do I change my lonely status when the
Very moment another heart is let into my world,
Hurt is the only exasperating feeling felt?
What am I doing wrong? So many unanswered questions.

Too afraid to love again.....

Why allow interest to become interested enough in me,
To the point of being lead to approach the fire which burns;
Deep within my soul, only to put out the flames; once there,
With your own selfish desires and tendencies? Does not,
How I feel inside matter to you? Do you not know how much
It hurts to be ignored after opening your heart to what
Turns out to be coldness? How many times must prayer;
Save me from loneliness and feelings of despair?
So many unanswered questions? What am I doing wrong?
Too afraid to love again.....

Victory Has Been Won

It's okay to cry;
When life has let you down.
No matter how hard you try;
On your face is left a frown.

And it's okay to cry;
When all hope is gone.
When questions of asking why;
Leaves you feeling alone.

So go ahead and cry, cry, cry!
Let the tears pour from your eyes!
But remember when you're done;
Victory has been won!

Yes, it's okay to cry;
When others have let you down!
No matter how hard you try!
No joy can be found.

And it's okay to cry
When all hope is gone.
No matter how hard you try;

You feel so sad and alone...

So go ahead and cry, cry, cry!
It's okay, cry, cry, cry!
Let the tears pour from your eyes!
Go ahead and cry....

But remember when you're done;
Victory has been won!

Thank You Jesus!
Thank You Jesus!
Thank You Jesus!
Victory has been won!

WHEN IT COMES TO SERVING THE LORD

I would rather be hot than cold
Don't want to be lukewarm
When it comes to serving the Lord
When it comes to serving the Lord

I would rather give one hundred percent
Can't give anything less
When it comes to serving the Lord
When it comes to serving the Lord

I believe I can achieve anything
If I keep my hands in the Master's plan
Cause I am not afraid
To stand on my faith
When it comes to serving the Lord
When it comes to serving the Lord!

WHERE YOU ARE

Lord, I desire;
To have a relationship with You!
One where there is no question;
About if Your love is true!
A unity filled;
With joy and possibility,
From a foundation built;
With trust and honesty!

Lord, I desire;
To give You all of my heart!
To fill it with Your presence;
As peace is its guard!
To walk hand and hand,
Beneath the moon, sun and stars.
I would walk forever,
Just as long as I'm where You are!

Cause to be where You are; Lord,
Means blessings shall be there,
Yes, to be where You are, Lord,
Means there shall live no fear!
Just real admiration and appreciation;

For the way, You show me You care!

Lord, I desire, to be where You are!
Yes, Lord! I desire, to be where You are!
Oh, where You are! Yes, where You are!
Lord, I desire, to be where You are!

You Deserve All Of My Praise

For delivering me, Yes Lord!
For teaching me, Yes Lord!
For setting me free, Yes Lord!
You deserve all of my praise!

For healing me, Yes Lord!
For saving me, Yes Lord!
For forgiving me, Yes Lord!
You deserve all of my praise!

Every day I wake;
I shall lift Your name up higher!
With every step I take;
Lord, I shall lift Your name up higher!
With every step I make;
Lord, I shall lift Your name up higher!
You deserve all of my praise!
Lord, You deserve all of my praise!

YOUR AMAZING GRACE

Lord I am here today,
Because You kept me.
When I was going through
You Lord, never left me.

Almost lost my mind
But You came in right on time,
And now I can't stop giving You praise
For Your Amazing Grace!

Your Amazing Grace,
Is the reason I'm still here today!
Giving all of my praise;
To Your Amazing Grace!

You can contact and find more information on

Dorothy A. Cooper

At:

katrinasworks.com

www.ingramcontent.com/pod-product-compliance
Lightning Source LLC
Chambersburg PA
CBHW060427050426
42449CB00009B/2166